Sussex as she wu

A Guide to the Sussex Dialect

Tony Wales

S. B. Publications

First published in 2000 by S B Publications
19 Grove Road, Seaford, Sussex BN25 1TP
01323 893498
Reprinted 2000
Reprinted 2001
Reprinted 2002

© 2000 Tony Wales

ISBN 1 85770 209 3

Drawings by Helen Fenton
Typeset by JEM Lewes
Printed and bound by
Tansleys the Printers
19 Broad Street
Seaford
East Sussex BN25 1LS
01323 891019

Front Cover: *Haymaking at Ashington.*
Title page: *Sheep washing at Lavant.*

Contents

Introduction

FIRST we should perhaps try to define what is dialect, and what is the difference between dialect and accent. As a general rule, Sussex dialect consists of old-fashioned words, most of which have ceased to be in general use, although this may not always be the case. It is impossible to say when dialect words were first used and, of course, their creation has been a continuous process. The period we are most concerned with has to be the years before universal schooling was complete, as it was the schools and, later, the wireless, which effectively brought the use of dialect words to an end.

Pyecombe hook

The collection of these old words is a fascinating pursuit, although it is fraught with difficulties and contradictions. Obviously, some of the words were in fairly general use, but many others circulated merely in one part of the county more than others. There are also many words which belong specifically to certain towns, villages or trades – and even particular families, or just to children.

However, that is not entirely the whole picture, as dialect is also often used to mean the way words are used, and the speaker's accent.

There was undoubtedly a definite Sussex accent, although even this varied across

Rottingdean shepherd Steve Barrow

the county. The typical Sussex manner of speaking has an attractive sing-song quality, with the words rising and falling as the speaker proceeds. To me, this manner of speech, coupled with the use of many archaic words, produces a most pleasant sound, although no doubt some will disagree.

The use of many dialect words continued even after the distinctive accent began to disappear. My parents, especially my mother, used many dialect words. In fact I grew up with them, and was shocked and surprised when I started school to find that others did not share these words. But I do not think anyone would have considered that either of my parents had a real Sussex accent. My grandparents were a different matter, as they not only used many old words, but also had a very distinctive Sussex sound to their speech.

Lewes Garland Day
1883

When I first began to collect Sussex dialect words, I was surprised to find how people's memories differed, although they may have been brought up during the same period. Some folk had no knowledge of dialect, while others accepted it as a definite part of their childhood. Obviously one's social status had a lot to do with this. The well-to-do families would have been quicker to adopt modern ways of speaking, looking upon the older dialect words as out of date and rather common. I have also been aware of a certain amount of disagreement over dialect words and their meanings. This seems perfectly natural, given all the circumstances, although some have queried why it should be that the words I recalled were completely unknown to them, or why the meanings I quoted were different from their own. All of this highlights the problems that face anyone trying to bring any kind of logical order into the fascinating world of Sussex dialect.

This little book is an attempt not only to explain many dialect words, but also to delve into the treasures of old Sussex sayings, rhymes and even certain foods. It is also a chance to pay tribute to some of the early dialect collectors and speakers, such as Richard Lower, his son Mark Antony Lower, the Reverend WD Parish and WG Daish. Mention should also be made of Margaret Wyndham who wrote the wonderful Sussex tales featuring Mrs Paddick, which included much authentic Sussex dialect. These appeared regularly in the *West Sussex Gazette* week by week, and have continued to be popular to this day, with the old series of stories being repeated many times.

The pursuit of Sussex dialect words and sayings is a continuing activity as far as I am concerned, so I will be delighted to have any additions, corrections or comments which readers may care to send me via the publisher.

Tony Wales
2000

Dictionary of Sussex dialect

Dialect words were often pluralised by added 'esses'. For instance: *Three little ghostesses, sitting on postesses, eating bread and toastesses, fighting with their fistesses.*

A

A-bear – To put up with something or someone. *I never could a-bear him.*

A-bed – Lying in bed, perhaps due to illness.

Abide – To put up with something.

Ad-as-leave – I would as soon as.

Adle – Unwell.

Adone – Leave off. *Oh do adone.*

Afeared – Afraid.

Afore – Before.

Agin – Close to. *Put that agin the wall.*

All-one – The same. *It's all-one to me.*

Allow – To give an opinion.

All-manner – To describe something as unsatisfactory, or just to end a sentence.

Allus – Always.

All mops and brooms – To be in a muddle.

Along-of – Because of.
Ammots – Ants.
Amost – Almost.
Ampre-ang – A decayed tooth.
Anywhiles/anywhen – At any time.
Apse – Close.
Arney – In a bad temper.
Arse-ackards – Backwards.
Arse-uppards – Upside down.
Arseholes – Medlars
Arts-and-parts – In all directions.
Aslew or asquif – In all directions.
As lief – I would as soon as.
Atween or atwixt – Between.
Awk – A big, ungainly person.
Axey – The ague, a dreaded complaint in old Sussex.

Ammot

ℬ
Bacca – Tobacco.
Bachelor's button – Pink campion.
Bad-abed and worse-up – Unwell.

Ballet – A song.
Balsam – Uncomplimentary remarks.
Bandy-ann day – Monday, the day for cold leftovers.
Bannick – A severe beating.
Bark – Bad cough.
Barse-ackards – Back to front.
Bat – Walking stick or some other piece of wood.
Bat and trap – A game played on Good Friday.
Bat-man – Smuggler's guard.
Beant – I'm not.
Beasted – Tired out.

Bat and trap

Beat the Devil round the gooseberry bush – To ramble on without getting to the point.
Beazled – Tired out.
Beer babies – Babies sired when the man was in drink.
Beggar-boy's heart – A very hard thing.
Beggar's broth – see Kettle broth.
Behopes – Let's hope.
Beleft – Believe.

Belikes – Likely.
Benson's pig – The floor or the ground.
Bettermost – Best quality or the best way.
Betwixt and between – Between one thing and another.
Biggest land and the worst reap – Said of someone full of woe.
Biggest part of a tidy bit – A fair amount.
Bile – To boil.
Birchbroom in a fit – Someone of rough appearance.
Biscuit – Cake.
Bishop Barnaby – Ladybird as used in children's rhyme.
Bittenous – Something liable to bite.
Bittle-battle – Stoolball.
Bizzum – Besom broom or naughty girl.
Black man – Imaginary monster or the Devil.
Black-eyed Susan – Sussex Pond or Well Pudding.
Blackthorn winter – Cold snap at the time of blackthorn
  blossom.
Block ornaments – Butcher's scraps.
Boco – A large amount.
Bodge – A careless job.
Boffled – Baffled.

Bishop Barnaby

Bon – Very good.
Bostal or borstal – Steep path.
Bottley – Glass marble from the neck of a bottle.
Boy's bacca – Wild clematis.
Brass love and copper compliments – Words of an untrustworthy person.
Brave – In good health.
Bread and cheese – Hawthorn shoots.
Bread and cheese friend – A true friend.
Bren-cheese – Bread and cheese.
Brish – To hurry up.
Broom-dasher – A rough person.
Brown George – A large apple turnover.
Brung – Brought.
Bum-freezer – A short coat.
Bumble cake – Cake made with honey.
Bumblesome – Clumsy.
Bunt – A blow.
Burny – Dry and brittle.

Boy's bacca

Butter and eggs – Birds-foot trefoil (also shoes and stockings, and lady's fingers).
By-the-bye – Accidentally or by chance.

C

Cabbage – To copy from another, as in an examination.
Cackhanded – Awkward person.
Cad – An inferior who helps you at work.
Caddling – Looking around for odd jobs.

Steam threshing at Woodingdean in the 1920s

Cadger – Beggar.
Call – Cause. *There's no call to speak like that.*
Called over – Reprimand.
Campion's eyebrows – Bushes on the side of Wolstonbury Hill.
Cannons – Game in which marbles are rolled along the gutter.
Cant whistle and eat flour – Cannot do the impossible.
Cardingly – Accordingly.
Cart – Left in the lurch. *He left me praply in the cart.*
Cat and conjure – Game, see Bat and trap.
Caterwise – Diagonally.
Catlicks – Roman Catholics.
Catterning – To beg for apples or money on St Catherine's Day.
Cavings – Ears raked off corn when it is threshed.
Chank – To chew.
Charlie – Fox.
Chastise – Correct or verbally abuse someone.
Cheese-cutter – Conker with flat edge, or a flat cap.
Chipe – To talk.
Chipper – Happy.
Chog – Apple core.
Chuckle-headed – Of low intelligence.

Chuff – Miserable or surly. The opposite of the modern term *chuffed*.
Chummy – Felt hat once worn by farm labourers.
Church bawled – Banns of marriage.
Church-yarder – Bad cough.
Clawneys – Family relations.
Clemmed – Hungry or cold.
Clobber – Clothes or belongings.
Close view of the floor – Spanking.
Cluck – To be self-satisfied (although Parish says 'out of spirits').
Clung – Cold and damp, such as damp washing.
Coager cake – A plain cake.
Cocker-up – To make up a story.
Coddy – Small and neat.
Coger or cojer – Meal of bread, cheese and beer.
Cold as charity – Very cold.
Come-by-chance – Illegitimate child.
Conk – Old piece of machinery, or to break down.
Consarned in liquor – Drunk.
Contrairy – Obstinate.
Cotch – Catch.
Countable – Very. *He is countable tight-fisted.*

Cowpat – Cow's droppings.
Crack nuts – Hazel nuts.
Create – To make a fuss.
Crossways – Where four roads meet.
Crow – To swank or boast.
Crundel – Ravine.
Cut your stick/hook – Be off straight away.

D

Crack nuts

Dabs – Game of knuckle-bones.
Dabster or dab hand – One who is good at something.
Dabtoe – Troublesome person.
Daddy-headed – One who is stupid.
Daft-cuddy – A simple person.
Daisy cutter – Penny farthing cycle, or cricket ball
  bowled low.
Dame – Respectful title given to aged woman, often a widow.
Dander – Temper. *He got my dander up.*
Dang – Alternative for damn, or something even worse.
Dare – May do something. *They dare to go outside.*
Darks – Moonless nights.

15

Darn-ma-wig – Expression of surprise.
Darter – Daughter.
Dasent – Clean and decent.
Deaf adder – Slow worm.
Deedy – Deep in thought.
Dencher – Field with the grass burnt off.
Delser – Small, neat article.
Dentical – Choosy.
Devil – Black lamb in a flock.
Devil dodgers – Those who go to church in the morning and chapel in the evening, or the other way about.
Devil's box – Church organ or harmonium, or some other reed musical instrument.
Devil's children – Magpies.
Devil's dancing hour – Very late.
Devil's prayer book – Pack of playing cards.
Dewlap – Early morning spider's web.
Dezzick – A day's work.
Dibs – Game of knuckle bones.
Dick – Ditch.

Devil's child

Dick or Dickie – Small boy, name unknown.
Didicais or diddies – Gypsies.
Dido – Mix-up.
Dinlow – Slow-witted.
Dishabill – Disorder.
Dish of tongues – A good telling-off.
Dishwipe or dishlick – Pied wagtail.
Ditch water – Something dull or miserable.
Dobbers – Marble game, see Cannons.
Dobbs or Master Dobbs – Fairy who helps with housework.
Doddle – Slow walk.
Doddle to-and-again – Walk to and fro.
Dog tail – Running about and getting in the way.
Dog tired – Tired out.
Dolly – Figure made of straw, or smallest pig in a litter.
Dollop – A lump of something.
Donkey tea – Drink made with toast crumbled in water.
Dont stoop down and pick up nothing – Don't do something unnecessary.
Doolah tap – Silly.
Doorstep – Large slice of bread.
Dorm – To move around in an annoying way.

Dosset – Small portion.
Dowly – Dreary.
Dozzle or dossle – Small article.
Dracy – Directly. *I'll do it dracly.*
Draggle tail – Sluttish girl.
Drinted or drented – When colours run in the wash.
Dripped (dropped) pudding – Suet pudding made to eat with the Sunday roast.
Drugged – Partly dry washing.
Druv – Driven.
Duck's Frost – Cold rain rather than freezing.
Dumbledore – Bumble bee.
Dunnamany or dunnamuch – Don't know how many or how much.
Dunner – Something not understood.
Dursn't – Must not.
Duzzick or dezzick – Hard day's work.
Dyke – Bank or ditch, also applied to a wc.

##

Eat enough to sink a barge and drink enough to float it again – eat and drink to excess.
E'en a most – Almost.
Effet – Newt.

Elynge – Weird or lonely.
Ether – Underwood of a hedge.

Effet

F

Faggot – Someone who is troublesome
  (Good-for-nothing girl, Parish says).
Faggot above a load – Too much of a
  good thing, or said of someone who was poor, but pretended otherwise.
Fainites – Call for truce.
Fair to middlin' – Slightly unwell
Fairy loaf – Fossilised sea urchin.
Farcey – Overeating.
Fardy – Interrupting. *Stop poking your fardy in*.
Farisees – Fairies.
Fat Jack – Fat or annoying person.
Fidgety Britches – Irritating person.
Fill-dick or fill-dyke – To fill with rain as in February fill dyke.
Fives – See Dabs.
Fla'ed Isaac – Unkempt person.
Flag basket – Basket woven from sedge.
Flasket – Basket.

The Alexandra Quoit Club team at Worthing c1900

Fleed cakes – Cakes made with pig's fat.
Flittermouse – Bat.
Flowering – Gathering wild flowers.
Flu – Delicate.
Follow after – Marble game, see Cannons.
Foreigner – Someone from elsewhere, even a neighbouring village.
Fraidy cat – Coward.
Frame – Person sick or ill.
Frap – To hit.
Freed – Very cold.
Frenchy – Foreigner.
Frit – Frightened.
Frouden – Frightened.
Frowsty – Stale air.
Fur my heel – To annoy.
Furrin – Foreign.
Furs bush – The cat's tune when purring.
Furze – Wheatear
Fust – First.

Marble players in The Street, Framfield, c1910

G

Gammy leg (or any other joint) – Injured limb.

Ganzie – Cardigan.

Gape seed – You are sowing gape seed if you are gazing out of the window.

Gaskin – Wild cherry.

Geat – Gate.

Gellish ornary – To feel ill.

Generally always – *He generally always does it that way.*

Gentleman – Someone who does not work for a living. Can be applied to an invalid or even a pet.

Gifts – White specks on fingernails.

Gill – Long stripe of woodland with a stream.

Gimsy – Well dressed.

Girt – Large.

Glim – A glimpse, or a ghost.

Goblins – A call after midday on Good Friday, when the marble season ends.

God Almighty's cow – Ladybird.

Goistering – Loud feminine laughter.

Gooding or Goodening – Custom of calling at big houses for gifts on St Thomas's Day, December 21.

Good length – Well kept garden.

Goodman – Old form of address for the man of the house.
Goody – Old form of address for a widow.
Gowk – A cuckoo, therefore a fool.
Grammered – Very dirty.
Gravel rash – Mark caused by falling on a gravel path or road.
Grisping and griping – Complaining.
Gurt or gert – Big.
Guttery alleys – Marble game, see Cannons.
Gwain – Going.

ℋ
Habern – Fireback.
Hagridden – To experience a nightmare.
Hagtrack – Circles of bright green grass, said to be tracks of dancing witches or fairies.
Halve – Long chat.
Ham – Grass plot.
Hanger – Wood on a hillside.
Happen along – Chance meeting.
Hard dick – Pudding made with flour and water.
Hard tack – Poor food.

A gowk

Harth money – Beer money.
Hassock – Matted vegetation.
Hasty pudding – Pudding made with bay leaves, eggs and milk.
Hayt – Carter's command to pull.
He – The Devil (or the main player in a tag game).
Heavy cake – Plum heavy.
Heart – Condition of land.
Heave gate – Gate that lifts out.
Hedge-pig – Hedgehog.
Heft – Lift.
Hem – Hell.
Herder – Udder.
Higgler – Hawker; in Heathfield, a chicken fattener.
High-lows –Footwear between shoes and boots.
Hill – Sussex Downs.
Hind – Servant.
His'n – His own.
Hobblyguts – Omnibus.
Hoggins – See Goblins.
Hoggle – To fall.
Hollerds – Dead branches.

Holt – Hold.
Holy Sunday – Easter Day.
Hopping John – Savoury soup, poured on bread.
Horn fair – Rough music intended to show disapproval of a neighbour.
Hot needle and a burning thread – Something done in a hurry.
Howlers – Men and boys who wassail the fruit trees.
Howsomdever – Summing up.
Huck – Pea-pod.
Huckle bones – Bones used in playing Dabs or Dibs.
Huckle-my-buff – Beer with eggs and brandy.
Hugger-mugger – A mess.
Humbledores – Hornets.
Huvver – Fluffed up.

I
Ibidioy – A lout.
Idle – Saucy.
Ikey – Proud, haughty.
Illify – To accuse someone.
Innards – The stomach.

Humbledore

Itchells – A lot of something.
Itching berries – Rose hips.
Item – A hint or clue.

J

Jackdaws' Parliament – Many talking at once.
Jack-hearns – Herons.
Jack in (or by) the hedge – Red campion.
Jacket – A good telling-off.
Jack on the pinch – Making use of someone.
Jacks – See Dabs.
Jack-up – To stop work.
Jacob – Starling.
Jambreads – Slices of bread and jam.
January butter – Sussex mud.
Jawmedead – A great talker.
Jib – Someone's manner or style.
Jigger – Harmless oath.
Jiggered – Surprised.
Jipper – Gravy.
Joe Bassetts – Larvae of the chafer beetle.

Jack-hearn

Jobal – Jolly.
Joe and 'Arry – Bread and cheese.
Jollop – Gravy or medicine.
Jonnick – Pleasant.
Joram – Large container.
Josser – Old fellow.
Joutering – Useless argument
Jump and hang by nothing – To do something in
  a hurry.
Juniper – Flea.
Justabout – Certainly.
Justly – Absolutely right.

Juniper

K

Keeps a good length – Keeps a good garden.
Kettle broth – Bread with pepper and salt in hot water.
Kettle wedges – Small pieces of wood suitable for the fire.
Kicks – Marble game involving throwing a marble against the side of one's boot.
Kiddle or kittle – To tease.
Kiddy – Friend or workmate.
Kime or kine – Weasel.

Kingcups – Marsh marigolds.
Kissing crust – Soft crust from middle of cottage loaf.
Kissing gate – Gate which can be used by just one person at a time.
Kiss me – Wild heartease.
Kite – Untidy person.
Kittle – Kettle.
Knabbler – One who gabbles.
Knap, nebb or knep – Small hill.
Knucker holes – Ponds reputed to be bottomless.

L

Laines – Open tracks of land at base of the Downs.
Lame – Any injury to arm or leg.
Lamentable – Very.
Lanky Tom – Very tall person.
Lapsy – Slow, lazy or stupid.
Lardy-johns – flat pastry cakes.
Large – Warm.
Larn – To teach or punish.
Larrup – A thrashing.
Latchety – Working poorly.

Smugglers' horses being auctioned outside the George Hotel, Crawley

Lather or leather – To thrash.
Laurence or Old Laurence – Mysterious person who makes one lazy.
Lawyers – Brambles.
Lay – Believe. *I lay that he spoke the truth.*
Lear – Feeling of emptyness in pit of stomach.
Leben – Eleven.
Leavebe – Let me.
Leaze – Land on which right of pasturage applies.
Leg – Long strip of land between woods or fences.
Leg-bail – To get away quickly.
Let be – To leave alone.
Levenses – Mid-morning snack.
Lew – Sheltered from the wind.
Libbet – Stick used for knocking fruit out of trees (also used for throwing at cocks and squirrels).
Licker – Something which takes a lot of believing.
Liddle – Little.
Liefer – Sooner.
Like – Often added to the end of a sentence.
Lil-ole – Adjective for almost anything.
Linger-and-Die – Horsham to Steyning railway line.

Lippy – Saucy.
Liversick – Hangnail.
Lodge – To lie flat.
Loiter-pin – Applied to a lazy person. *He would make a loiter-pin to wind down the sun.*
Lone-handed – Single-handed.
Longanner – Tall person.
Long hook – A long time to wait. *On a long hook.*
Long Rope Day – Good Friday, from the custom of skipping on this day.
Looby – Stupid.
Lord John or Old Johnny – The ague.
Lords and ladies – Wild arum.
Lord Tom Noddy – An important person in his/her own estimation.
Lot, lote – Pond.
Loute – To bend.
Loving mud – Sussex mud. *Becus it do cling so.*
Low – Allow or conclude.
Lubbock – Big ungainly person

Long Rope Day on Brighton beach

Luddick – Something which has fallen down.
Lurgy – Lacking in energy or an un-named illness.
Lydes – Lower slopes of a hill.

M

Magnify – Matter. *It don't magnify one way or t'other.*
Maid – Young child of either sex.
Main – Much.
Malook – Mad or daft.
Marble Day – Good Friday.
Mare's tails – Streaky white clouds.
Mariandums – Marks rather than writing.
Marmish – Tasteless flavour
Master – Old name for a married man, or wife for her husband.
Mawk – Sluttish girl.
Maybe, mayhap – Perhaps.
Mazed – Bewildered.
Meece – Mice.
Melancholy – Much.
Mermaid's purses – Egg cases of the dog fish.
Merry – Wild cherry.

Messpot – Dithering person.
Middlin' – Word used when the speaker does not wish to commit himself.
Milkmaids – Ladies smock.
Mind – Remember.
Miriander – A happy halfwit.
Mis or mus – Shortened form of Mister.
Misagree – To disagree.
Miserable – Mean.
Miserable as sin – Very depressed.
Mislike – Dislike.
Mister Grim – The Devil.
Mistus – Mistress.
Misword – A cross word.
Mizmaze – Confused state.
Mock-beggar hall – House or farm where food and furnishings are poor.
Moggy – Barn own, or a cat.
Moithered – Bewildered.
Monkey's birthday – When it rains and the sun shines at the same time.

South Down shepherd and his dog looking towards Ditchling, c1930s

Month of Sundays – Long and boring time.
Monstrus – Very much.
Morris or morrising – To dance.
Mort – Many.
Most-in-ginral – Usually.
Mousearnickle – Dragonfly.
Mouzle – To crumple up.
Mumpers – Tramps.
Mush-faker – Poorly dressed person.
Music – Any musical instrument, but particularly
  a concertina or melodeon.
Muther-wut – Carter's command to a horse to turn right.
Mutton Barracks – Valley near Telscombe noted for its sheep.
My obediance – Mother's name for her first born.

N

Mousearnickle

Nary – Not any.
Naughty man's plaything – Stinging nettle.
Naythur – Neither.
Near – Miserly.
Neat – Exact.

Neddie – Warble fly.
Nestle – To fidget.
Nettle – To annoy.
Nettle beer – Drink made from nettles.
Nine times round a cabbage (or bush) – Long time getting to the point.
Nineways-for-Sunday – To look surprised.
Nipper – Young boy.
No chicken – Not so young.
No nation thing – Expression of scorn.
No-one-wheres – Nowhere.
Not blown away – Not short of money.
Nottable – Thrifty.
Nupe – Foolish person.
Nuzzle – Nestle.

O

Oakam – Nonsense.
Obediance – A bow.
Ockerd – Awkward.
Old apple woman – A ditherer.
Old Clem – Figure set over the place where blacksmiths held their St Clement's Day feast on November 23.

Old faggot – Troublesome person.
Old fashioned – Suspicious look.
Old fashioned touch – Old style person.
Old Grist – Very fat. *As fat as Old Grist.*
Old man's beard – Wild clematis.
Old man's nightcap – Hooded bindweed.
Old Steere's pig – Answer to question – Who said that?
Old Tom Pepper –Very great liar. *As big a liar as Old Tom Pepper.*
On – Of. *I tried to grab hold on 'em.*
On pins – To be worried.
Oration – A fuss.
Ornary – Unwell.
Orts – Bits and pieces.
Othergates – Other ways.
Otherwheres – Other places.
Otherwhiles – Other times.
Ought about nought –To say nothing.
Ourn – Ours.
Outermost – Greatest.
Overlay – Oversleep.

Over Will's mother's – Tucked away in some place, or used to indicate direction of bad weather.
Owler – Smuggler.

P

Paddle – To walk around indoors with muddy shoes.
Painful – Painstaking.
Parley Francey – To speak French or some other foreign language.
Particular – To appear to be unwell.
Passel – Large group.
Pawsy – Stupid.
Peaky – Looking sickly.
Peewits – Small marbles.
Peert – Lively.
Peg away – Carry on working.
Pemsy – Pevensey.
Personable – Charming.
Pert – Pretty.
Peter-Grievous – Whining child.
Pharisees – Fairies.
Pickle – Pitchfork.

Picksome – Finicky.
Pig meat – Pork.
Pig nut – Earth nut.
Pig sticker – Large knife.
Piker or pikey – Tramp.
Pill garlic – Something hot.
Pimps – Bundles of firewood.
Pinch Bottom Day – May 29.
Pinchplumb – Mean person.
Pinchgut – Relieving officer.
Plagey – Troublesome.
Plaster for every wound – Answer for every problem.
Pleasuring – An outing.
Pletty – Irregular.
Plim – To rise up.
Plum heavy – Round pastry cake made with currants.
Poke – Sack.
Pond pudding – Sussex pudding or well pudding.

Pharisees

Pooch – Pout or push.
Pook – Punch, as in beggar-pooker. Also a fairy name.
Pooking stick – Billiard cue.
Pook flies – Fairy flies.
Pook-noodle – Muddler.
Poor man – The Devil.
Poor man's treacle – Garlic.
Poundnotish – Well spoken.
Prapper – Proper.
Prensley or preddenly – Presently or at present.
Prickleback urchin – Hedghog.
Prodidogs – Protestants.
Puck – Nightjar.
Pucker – A fuss, or snatched with cold.
Pucksie – Rotten.
Puck stool – Toadstool.
Puff – A lifetime.
Pug up – Put a thing away safely.
Purling – Looking intently.
Purty – Pretty.
Puss net – Tangled string.

Puck stool

Sussex men wunt be druv

Q

Quality – The nobility.
Quarry – Small window glass.
Queer – To puzzle. *It queers me.*
Quick – Pregnant or alive.
Quid – A cud.
Quiddy – What did you say?
Quidsing – Doing well.
Quissby – Unsettled weather.

R

Rackon – Reckon.
Radical – Bad or troublesome.
Ragtush – Untidy person.
Rake – Applied to the sea when it breaks on the beach.
Rake – Thin. *As thin as a rake.*
Ramp – To grow rapidly.
Rare – Good, plentiful.
Rat Dick – River Arun at Horsham.
Rathe – Early or soon.
Rattle-banger – Noisy vehicle.

Raw throat – Sore throat.
Rawt and rawtun – Angry complaining.
Red-headed Dane – Red-headed man.
Reynolds or Reynard – Fox, often Mus Reynolds.
Rheumatics – Rheumatism.
Rindy frost – Hoar frost.
Roaders – Tramps.
Rook – Swindle.
Rookery – Disturbance or place where a crowd gathers.
Rough music – Sounds made by tin pans, horns etc to express social disapproval of person or persons.
Round frock – Often used for a smock, although the two are slightly different.
Rousers – Large fireworks associated with Lewes, also rook scarers.
Rubbishy-buster – Very untidy person.
Rumbustical – Blusterous.
Runagate or runagit – Good for nothing person.
Runaway jack – Ground ivy.

Sussex smock worn by Cyril Phillips of Firle, c1950s

S

Sad – Cakes or bread not risen.
Sarternoon – This afternoon.
Sartinly – For certain.
Scandalise – Insult someone.
Scads – Small black plums.
Scattel – Troublesome person.
Schmosell – Lot of noise or fuss.
Scholard – Scholar.
Scorse – To exchange.
Scrabbles – See Goblins.
Screws – Rheumatism.
Scritch owl – Barn owl.
Scroopun – whistling merrily.
Scrumping – Stealing fruit from trees.
Scrouging – Pushing.
Scurriwinkle – To move furtively.
Scutty – A wren.
Sen – Since.
Seraphim – Church barrel-organ.
Sessions – A fuss.

Set-out – Mix-up.
Setter – Broody hen.
Settle – Wooden bench.
Shab – To hurry.
Shackle – Thin vegetable soup, or to idle.
Shackle-britches – Slow person.
Sheeres – The country apart from Sussex and Kent.
Shepherd's crown – Fossil sea urchin.
Shepherd's ganzer or ganzie – Coat worn by farm
  workers.
Shimeroys – Gnats.
Ship – Sheep.
Shirty – Bad-tempered.
Shock – Sheaf of corn.
Shoon – Shoes.
Shooting Alley – Large marble.
Shorn bug – Beetle.
Short – Bad-tempered, or pastry that is crumbly.
Short shoes and long corns – A curse for your enemy.
Shruck – Shrieked.
Shun – Shove.

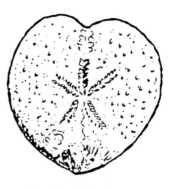

Shepherd's crown

Shut of – To be rid of someone or something.
Side hill – Hillside, particularly the Downs.
Skattle cat – Woman of sly disposition.
Skidders (skiddaws, skellers, skeelers, skimmers) – Piece of metal used by children to control a hoop.
Skillings – Low roofed rooms, sloping to the ground.
Skin – One's temper. *He's in a bad skin.*
Slew-ways – Sideways.
Slirrup – Suck up noisily.
Slommocky or slummocky – Messy or untidy.
Slop – Shepherd's jacket.
Slouch-puddin – Shambling walker.
Slyboots – Sly, devious person.
Smell of an oil rag – To give nothing away. *I wouldn't give him a smell of an oil rag.*
Smugs – Word said at midday on Good Friday when playing marbles.
Snag or sneg – Snail.

Good Friday marbles at Battle

45

Haymaking with oxen

Snags – See Goblins.
Snottgogs – Yew berries.
So drunk he couldn't see through a ladder – Very drunk.
Soodle – Loiter.
Soon – Daft or slow-witted.
Spad-lashes – Leggings.
Spannel – To make dirty foot marks on a clean floor.
Sparticles – Spectacles.
Spat – A slap.
Spik – Speak.
Spile – Spoil.
Spiramawgus – Name used to frighten children.
Spotted dick or dog – a sultana sponge pudding.
Sprod – Junction of branch with trunk of tree.
Spruse or spruser – To cheek or mislead, and one who is sly.
Spurtle – Porridge stirrer.
Squeeze-belly gate – Narrow gate.
Squatetings – Female conversation.
Squack – Baby's cry.
Squimbly – Feeling queer or upset.
Srievelous – Very slow.

Spurtle

Stampsies – Cry of conker-player as he stamps on opponent's conker.
Starving – Shooting at birds.
Stiver – To walk briskly.
Stone alleys – Stone marbles.
Stranger – A single tea-leaf floating in a cup of tea.
Strick – Strike.
Struttick – Nothing. *He hasn't got a struttick.*
Suky – Kettle.
Sunnuck – Something.
Surelye – Word often added to the end of a sentence to round it off.
Sussex bomb or Sussex gumbo – Sussex pond pudding.
Sussex moon – Lantern used at the back of a waggon.
Sussex pudding – Simple flour and water pudding.
Sussex weed – Oak.
Swanky – Light beer.

Sussex weed

Sweal – To singe, burn, also to scour clothes.
Swede-nawer or Sussex swede – Ignorant countryman.
Swimmers – Flat rounds of plain suet pudding boiled and served with treacle
  or jam. Also used to describe an unnappetising dish.
Swipes – Light beer.
Swymy – Feeling faint or sick.

$\mathcal{T}$

Tackle-to – Start a new job.
Take-and-go – Make up one's mind suddenly.
Tallyman – Door-to-door salesman who collects money weekly. Also used
  in hop-picking.
Tantaddlings – Small jam tarts.
Tanty – Dainty.
Tapsell gate – Gate working on a central pivot.
Tarade – A lot of noise or commotion.
Tarble – Terrible, much.
Tar-boy – Boy with a tar-pot at sheep-shearing, to use as an antiseptic on a cut.
  Don't spile the ship for a ha'porth of tar.
Tarrify – Terrify.
Taw – Large marble.

Alciston Court Farm in the early years of the last century.

Tea leaves – Siskins.
Tedious or tejus – Very. *It were a tejuss large amount.*
Tenterhooks, on – In suspense.
Terrify – Tease.
Tessy and Tiffy – Irritable.
Thick of hearing – Deaf.
Thunderbolt – Shepherd's crown (fossil).
Thwartled – Cross ploughed
Tibster – Small man.
Tight – In good heart.
Timmersome – Timid.
Timnails – Vegetable marrow.
Tinpot – Self-important person.
Tipteers or tipteerers – Christmas mummers.
Tissicky – Troublesome (cough).
Token – Gift or a ghost sent to warn of a death.
Toll – Clump of trees.
Tollard – Candle grease.
Toller – Tallow.
Tolly – Shooting marble.
Tom bacca – Traveller's joy.

Tooters – Seaside tradesmen.

Top of the house – To lose one's temper.

Tot – Tuft of grass or hair.

Tottle grass – Quaking grass.

Totty land – High land.

Trimmer – Naughty child.

Trip – To place something behind a wheel to prevent it slipping.

Trug – Sussex basket made of split wood.

Tumble-down gate – Gate opened by pressing down one end.

Turn-out – Confusion.

Turrble – Terrible.

Twit – To tease.

Twitten – Path between walls or buildings.

Twizzling – Spinning a pointer on a pub ceiling to decide who should buy the next round (or to divide up smuggled goods).

Tyke – A naughty child.

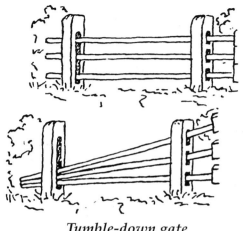

Tumble-down gate

U

Unaccountable – Very, or exceptional.

Unkid – Not made known.

Upright and downstraight – Honest, uncomplicated person. Also bedtime when the clock says six.

Upsides – Hard to get the better of.

Urchin – Hedgehog.

Urr – Rough taste, such as quince.

Utchy – Cold.

V

Valiant – Brave or very much.

Varmint – Rogue.

Varn – Bracken.

Varning – Collecting bracken.

Virgin's garlands – Chaplets of white flowers, sometimes used at the funerals of young women.

Voller – Fallow.

W

Walloping – Spanking.

Wapple way or waffle way – Bridle path.

Water bewitched – Very weak tea.

Weeson – Throat.

Well mannered – Describing the growth of vegetables.

Well pudding – Sussex pond pudding.

Wet – To make tea.

Wet week – Slow or dispirited. Slow as a wet week.

Wheelbarrow – Used instead of an unfamiliar word.

Whiffle – Coming in fits and starts.

Whistle and row (or ride) – Work while you talk.

Whittle – Cape or shawl.

Widdershins – Contrary to course of the sun.

Wig – A bun.

Wild – Weald.

Willick – Guillemot, also a wild person or an Eastbourne fisherman.

Wimwams for goose's bridles – Something not understood.

Wittle – Fringed shawl.

Woddle – The game of Bat and Trap.

Working for a dead horse – Working for a wage already received.
Worsle or worslers – Wassail or wassailers.
Wounded beanstick – Tall thin person.
Wrastle – Do battle with.
Wrocked – Wrinkled.
Wrop up – Wrap up against the cold.

Y

Yaffle – Green woodpecker.
Yappin' – Singing tunelessly.
You got up afore you went anywhere – You wasted time.
Yoster – Play roughly.

Willicks

A passel of trade words

Different trades and crafts have their own dialect words, some of which have survived, while others have been forgotten. Here are just a few examples, although I am sure that there must be many more still waiting to be collected.

Ackle – The working of a piece of machinery. *This is how it ackles.*
Axe-helve – Axe handle.
Bait – Farm worker's fare, such as bread and cheese or fat bacon, and cold tea.
Bat – Scythe handle.
Bodger – Chair maker, or a careless worker.
Cant – Alloted area for contract work (building trade).
Clutterdump – Rubbish dump.
Carroty – Brittle or crumbly wood.
Chicked ped – Crate to hold plucked birds for market.
Cochel – Too much for a wheelbarrow and not enough for a cart.
Cowman's bedsocks (also Wurlers, Yorkers) – Cord or strap used by farm labourer to raise his trousers.
Crowd – To take bricks off the hack and place them on a barrow.
Crowding – Preparing bricks in a clamp for burning.

Dibble, dibber, dibbler – Wooden tool for making holes to receive seeds.
Dryth – Damp soil.
Dungpot – Dung cart.
Duzzick, dezzick – Hard day's work.
Eddenbite – Mass of cloud in form of a loop (fishermen).
Egger-nogger – Sleet (fishermen).
Fettlers – Railway plate layers.
Fussell – Sickle.
Grunter – Misaligned course of brickwork.
Hack – Bank of earth (brick making).
Heart – Condition of land.
Hedge-carpenter – Rough worker.
Hogboat – Brighton fishing boat.
Hummucking – Digging clay to stack (brick-making).
Jug – Brighton fisherman.
Jugglers – Brighton fish carriers.
Latten – Sheep bell, or thin metal.
Looker – Shepherd.
Messengers – White clouds blown by the wind (fishermen)
Miller's glory or pride – Windmill sweeps set in the sign of a cross.
Mixen – Dungheap.

Sheep bells

Nims – See Cowman's bedsocks.
Nollegers – See Cowman's bedsocks
Ox bow – Wooden yoke for oxen.
Painter's lunch – Half a pint of
  beer and five Woodbines.
Peck – Pick axe.
Pig – Misaligned course of brickwork.
Planety – Calm with close, moist air (fishermen).

A mixen

Pork-bolters – Worthing fishermen.
Port-boys – Small low clouds in a clear sky (fishermen).
Prickles – Fish baskets holding a bushel.
Quarry – Small window glass.
Rack up – To give horses their nightly feed.
Rovendens – See Cowman's bedsocks.
Ruddles – Green wood interwoven between upright material to make a hedge.
Rumbler – sheep bell.
Running the hacks – Drying areas of new bricks.
Sear or sere – Dried grass. To burn or scorch.
Sheep drib or cage – Frame holding sheep's hay.

Stocks at Midhurst.

Punishment stocks at Midhurst early in the twentieth century

Shucky – Unsettled weather (fishing).
Skinte – To move bricks on to a drying rack.
Sledge – Blacksmith's hammer.
Smither diddles – Mock sun (fishing).
Sneathe or snead – Scythe handle.
Snirk – Dried, withered.
Soil – Fine ash (brick-making).
Spicket – Spigot.
Spread bats – Cross pieces used with horse teams.
Spud – Fork.
Stagging the old one – Watch out for the boss (brick-making).
Sussex marble – Winklestone.
Swallocky – Sultry weather (fishing).
Tackle – Working tools.
Teller – Man who throws fish on bench prior to counting.
Tooters – Seaside tradesmen.
Truggy – Dirty weather fishing).
Warp – Four herrings (two in each hand).
Wheels – Handcart or sack truck.
Windogs – White clouds blown by the wind (fishing).

Onery, twoery — counting in dialect

Although many shepherds and agricultural workers may have been relatively un-educated in the book-learning sense, they still had to be adept at keeping count of the animals in their charge. Barclay Wills, the Worthing writer on the South Downs scene, quotes an old time shepherd: 'Most times I used my crook-stick to cut the notches in, so I never lost my count. 'Tis a handy way if you beant much of a scholard. Pencil an' paper be good in their way too, but not as good as a stick and a knife; the notches is allus to hand, an' easy to remember.'

For more complicated counting, individual shepherds used sets of dialect words, which, although similar, often differed slightly from those used by their neighbours. This is a common set of numbers:

> *One-erum, Two-erum, Cockerum, Shu-erum, Shitherum,*
> *Shatherum, Wine-berry, Wagtail, Tarrydidle, Den.*

Usually the sheep were counted in pairs, so den stood for twenty. However, some other agricultural workers counted in multiples of five.

Here is another set which goes right up to twenty, with every fifth word accented.

> *Wintherum, Wontherum, Twintherum, Twontherum,*
> *Wagtail, Whitebelly, Coram, Dar, Diddle, Den,*
> *Etherum, Atherum, Shootherum, Cootherum,*
> *Windbar, Bobtail, Inadik, Dyadik, Bumpit, Ecack-tally.*

Another set may be missing some numbers:

> *Obery, Twoery, Tickory, Tebbon,*
> *Ollobone, Crackabone, Ten or Eleven,*
> *Spin, Span, Must-be-done, Twiddleum,*
> *wydleum, Twenty-one.*

Of course, some of these strange words were noted from older shepherds, whose memory could have been playing tricks. The following is a further set which seems to owe something to the last batch:

> *Onery, Twoery, Zickery, Zam.*
> *Holly, Bona, Cracker, Bone, Ninery.*
> *Ten, Strim, Stram, It, Must, Be, Dine,*
> *Twaddle, Um, Twaddle, Um, Twenty-one.*

Yet another set, similar to some of the foregoing, is quoted by Mrs J Duggan Rees in her book *Slindon: Portrait of a Sussex Village* (1988). Her informant was an old shepherd, George Bowley.

> *One the Rum, Two the Rum, Cocker Rum,*
> *Shutter Rum, Shether Rum, Shather Rum, Wim Berry,*
> *Wig Tail, Darry Diddle, Dess.*

Sussex was by no means the only county where dialect counting was in use and similar words have been noted from elsewhere in England. There were also dialect words used by children in their counting games. This set was collected in Sussex in 1935.

> *Ena, Deenah, Dinah, Doe.*
> *Catterah, Wheelah, Whiler, Whoa.*
> *Coram, Doram, Pullem, Flea.*

Three dialect greats

William Parish

There have been several distinguished collectors and speakers of Sussex dialect, but most will agree that the greatest of them all was the Reverend William Douglas Parish, who in 1875 published *A Dictionary of the Sussex Dialect*. Those fortunate to possess a copy of this book will assuredly agree that it is a scholarly work, but without a single dull page. His descriptions of old Sussex words, all of them collected from the folk themselves, are instructive but, at the same time, immensely entertaining. His book on Sussex words was followed by a similar volume for Kent Parish was the son of Sir Woodbine Parish, a distinguished diplomat, and for forty-one years he remained a country priest in Sussex. He was the first curate at Firle, and then became vicar for the parishes of Selmeston and Alciston. An enthusiast of cricket, he coached and played with great success. He was a skilled archaeologist, chairman of the Sussex Archaeological Society for eight years, and was the first person to transcribe the Domesday Book into modern English. His other interests included education – he was a much-loved school inspector – and gypsy lore.

The priest's youthful outlook endeared him to his parishioners, and particularly to children. Frank Holmes showed me a letter which Parish wrote to a little girl called Mary, in which he says: 'One of my cats, being kept indoors by the bad weather, has just got at my stuffed birds and eaten one. I hope it will make her ill.'

He always made a point of talking to his gypsy friends whenever they appeared at Selmeston. They appreciated his friendship and made a practice of taking their babies to him to be christened.

Dallington Mill in 1909

Rural scene at Telscombe village

He gave each baby a small Russian cross, which was worn as a kind of charm.

Among his many gifts was a keen sense of humour, although he did not have a very advanced musical taste. Once when visiting a neighbouring church he asked if the man tuning the organ could stop for a few minutes while he spoke to his fellow clergyman. He was told rather sharply that the organist was in fact in the middle of giving a recital. Probably this joke against himself was just the sort of story he delighted in telling when he was called upon to give one of his popular talks.

Parish's delightful book on Sussex dialect was originally published in Lewes in 1875 and later expanded and illustrated by Helena Hall and her brothers in 1957.

Here is an example from the later edition of Parish's book:

HEDGE CARPENTER. An old hedge carpenter worked for our brother at Uckfield from 1888 to 1891. He was named Benjamin Tunks and used to aver "Ye cah't cut a board 'zackly square ye know Sir, and my motter's 'Let nigh enough bide'." A favourite phrase was 'About so-ey'. He made and inlaid a workbox for his bride with forty different kinds of wood including broom and ling. When we praised it the old man said 'Aah! them wot knowed wot Oi cud do would'n beleef as 'ow Oi done oit, (a pause) but them wot seed me do it they beleft as 'ow Oi done it."

James Richards of Helsum (Hailsham), originally an itinerant preacher, was described as one of the most lovable recorders of the Sussex dialect in the early part of the twentieth century. He had many Sussex friends, and in his books, which are now collectors' items, he records his own particular love of Sussex and its people. One of his poems begins:

> 'Twos dunameny years agoo, dat
> Sussex cum to light.
> De hills wos wunce under de sea,
> and packed dere purty tight.

He died in 1949 at the age of eighty-three, having rendered his simple Christian principles into the authentic voice of Sussex. He printed his work on a hand-press and acted as his own publisher and distributor. One of his books is *De Good News according to Mark. Put into de Sussex Dialect by Jim Cladpole*. It was published in February 1936 and cost one shilling. This starts:

De beginning of de Good News of Saver de Anointed, de Son of God; As it can be written in de books of de tellers. "Lookye! I send My Messaager. And he shall clear de way afore Me. Harkye! One be calling: Clear ye in de common lands de futway of de Lord, Tread well down in de lonely plaaces a highway for our God. John token-washed folk in de common land and preached de token-washing of a chaanged mind to git rid of sins. And people from all over Judea and Jerusalem went out to him; and was token-washed by him in de river Jordan owning up to dere sins. John wore a camel's hair and had a leather belt round he's middle; and he's vittles was locustes and wild honey, and he cried saying, "Dere comes after me One who be more mighty dan I be, whose ha'boots I beant good enough to bend down and undo. Surely, I token-wash you wid water, but he will token-wash you wid de Holy Spirit."

Richard Lower, father of the better-known Sussex author Mark Antony Lower, was born at Alfriston and became the village schoolmaster at Muddles Green near Chiddingly. He wrote a fascinating book, *Stray Leaves from an Old Tree*, and also wrote dialect poems. Probably his best known work is *Tom Cladpole's Jurney to*

Lunnon and *Jan Cladpole's Trip to 'Merricur in search of Dollar Trees*.

These were published in Lewes in the early 1900s and remained in print for many years. They cost sixpence each.

Mark Antony Lower followed in his father's footsteps with several books, including dialect works, such as a version of *The Song of Solomon*. He was known particularly for his book *Contributions to Literature*, and his essay on the South Downs.

Here is a small taster of Richard Lower's *Jurney to Lunnon* (told by himself and written in pure Sussex doggerel by his Uncle Tim).

> *Last Middlemas, I 'member well, when harvest wos all over,*
> *Us cheps had hous'd up all de banes, an' stacked up all de clover.*
> *I think says I, I'll take a trip, to Lunnun, dat I wol,*
> *An see how things goo on a bit, lest I should die a fool.*
> *Fer Sister Sal, five years agoo, went off wud squyer Brown,*
> *Housemaid, or summat – dun know what, to live at Lunnon town.*

These two delightful little books are, naturally, no longer in print, but libraries will have them.

Crawley Fair a century ago

*S*ussex sayings and saws

You may push and you may shov
But I'm hemmed if I'll be druv.

This might be considered the unofficial motto of a true Sussex man. The lovely dialect word druv means, of course, driven. In other words, those of us who come from Sussex will not be made to do anything against our inclination. This obstinate trait in the Sussex character may be interpreted as a virtue, or a vice, depending on one's point of view. Certainly it exists, and I can point to many examples in my own family. My great-grandmother, a fearless country nurse, was noted both within and outside the family circle for her obdurate ways. Many stories circulated among her children and grandchildren, but only one must suffice. When Portuguese soldiers were billeted in Sussex during the First World War, one of them was brought home to tea by one of her teenage granddaughers. Gran barked at him: 'How's your mother?' The girl remonstrated with the old lady, saying he didn't understand. Gran's terse reply was: 'Surely he knows his own mother'. On my father's side of the family my grandfather was equally 'Sussex', and any attempt to persuade him to do a job before he was good and ready was always met with complete disregard.

My first Sussex book, published in 1976, was *We Wunt be Druv*, and although it has been out of print for many years, I am still asked for it; probably the title has something to do with this. The Sussex author Victor Cook included the word in one of his poems, ending each stanza with:

For Sussex will be Sussex, and Sussex won't be druv.

Sussex Genders

> *Everything in Sussex is a She*
> *except a Tom Cat, and she's a He.*

This strange inclination to use the feminine gender when speaking of all manner of things in Sussex persists to this day. However, I have been told that fields, ladders, axes, hooks and hoes are always masculine, although a scythe is always a she. Windmills, and the wind itself, are certainly feminine, as these lines on an old mill, noted by Mark Antony Lower, make plain:

The village pump at Ringmer

> *The mill she is built of wood, iron and stone.*
> *Therefore she cannot go aloan.*
> *Therefore to make the mill to go,*
> *The wind from some part she must blow.*

A Sussex menu

This list of the Seven Good Things of Sussex is often quoted, but is too fine to be omitted.

> *A Chichester lobster, a Selsey cockle,*
> *An Arundel mullet, a Pulborough eel,*
> *An Amberley trout, a Rye herring*
> *And a Bourne wheatear, are the best of their kind.*

A Sussex litany

I have no idea who penned these lines, but they sound like good sense.

> *From flints and sands and barren lands,*
> *Good fortune set me free.*

> *From sounds of guns, and women's tongues,*
> *Good Lord deliver me.*

A Sussex Toast

There are, of course, hundreds of these, many of them popular in the annual harvest suppers that were once held in Sussex villages. This is just one:

> *Yurr's to 'ee, may 'ee live till 'ee die.*
> *And may every hair of your 'ead be a candle to light 'ee to Glory.*

Some pieces of good advice

These old Sussex admonitions mostly speak for themselves.

> *Eat winkles in March – they are as good as a dose of medicine.*

> *Keep out of four houses – the inn, the work 'ouse, the infirmary and the prison.*

> *Sand on clay, never did pay.*
> *But clay on sand, is good for the land.*

Sand is washed through the clay but the other way round it will form a coating for loamy soil.

> *If you burn a Sussex man, watch out for the ashes.*

> *If you won't work in the heat, then you may have to go hungry when the frosts come.*

> *A brewer of mischief deserves to be drowned in his own mash tub.*

> *He who buys land, buys stones.*
> *He who buys flesh, buys bones.*
> *He who buys eggs, buys shells,*
> *But he who buys good ale, buys nothing else.*

> *Smuggler's gold doant wear*
> *(Ill-gotten cash doesn't last)*

> *An apple pie without the cheese is like a kiss without the squeeze.*

Yes, I know this is often claimed by other counties, but we said it first.

One boy is a boy. Two boys is half a boy. Three boys is no boy at all.

Anyone who has ever employed boys will know exactly what this means.

If I rest, I rust.
If I trust, I bust.
Therefore no rest, no rust.
No trust, no bust.

Counting crows

One crow for sorrow, two crows for joy.
Three crows for a letter, four crows for a boy.
Five crows for silver, and six crows for gold.

Cutting nails

Cut them on Monday, cut them for health.
Cut them on Tuesday, cut them for wealth.
Cut them on Wednesday, cut them for news.

> *Cut them on Thursday, a pair of new shoes.*
> *Cut them on Friday, cut them for sorrow.*
> *Cut them on Saturday, see your true love tomorrow.*
> *But cut them on Sunday, your safety seek*
> *Or the Devil will have you all the rest of the week.*

So often rhymes and saying spell out how unwise it was to do almost anything on Sunday, except perhaps attend church.

A weather saying

There were, of course, lots of these, but in Sussex – and other counties as well – one of the best known was a reference to the outlook appearing black 'over Will's mother's'. Nobody has come up with any explanation as to who Will was, although the phrase is still used.

Another expression was 'Min Upton's little ole Will' used when a particular name could not be recalled. Perhaps this was the same Will!

Nicknames

Nicknames were once extremely popular. Gilbert Sargent, whose memories of

Sussex country life were edited by Dave Arthur in *A Sussex Life* (1989), remarked that everyone seemed to have a nickname. some of those he remembered were Ossie Wright, Sneezer Bartholomew, Tinto Sheather and his father, Cocky Billy (because he was smart).

Henry Burstow, in his *Reminiscences of Horsham* (1911), quotes a great many nicknames in use in his day. Foot'em Jenkins (who had very short legs), Patch Price (who had a club foot, and was the last man to be punished in the Horsham stocks), Cherry Ripe (Charlotte Venn, mother of Hewett, the murderer) and Pin-Toe Nanny (who was sold by her husband at Horsham Fair).

Smugglers had nicknames among themselves, such as Towzer, Old Joll and Nasty Face.

I can remember several names from my own youth – Old Cop (the school teacher), Cass (the Catholic priest), Yorky (the outside porter) and Fishy (purveyor of fish and vegetables). Even my father had one – Galloper

Lardy Richardson, a Horsham character who was said to have been the last man in town to wear a Sussex smock. His nickname came from his occupation as an army cook.

Wales, apparently because he worked so fast and was not, therefore, always popular with the other men. My own nickname at school was Toenails.

To finish off, here are the words that were sometimes used by a singer at the end of his or her performance in a Sussex pub.

It's a good song, and very well sung.
And very good company, every one.
If you can beat it, you're welcome to try.
But always remember, the singer is dry.

Remember by rhyme

When a Sussex countryman of a century or more ago wished to remember something, it was more than likely that he included it in a rhyme. This was a useful way of recalling important bits of information or lore, and equally applicable whatever one's age. No television or radion, and often not even books, at least for the working folk, so rhymes and jingles were educational and enjoyable at the same time.

If youth but knew what age would crave,
How many a sixpence youth would save.

Imparting the knowledge of age started with tiny mites. My mother remembered the jaunty tunes to which arithmetic tables were chanted in her young days, and schooldays apart there were plenty of jolly little rhymes, with perhaps a serious undertone, for the youngsters to learn.

> *If ..... is a good little boy (or girl)*
> *And ..... is a dear one,*
> *He (or she) shall have a brand new coat (or any article)*
> *Made out of Mother's (or Father's) old one.*

Any item of clothing could be brought into the rhyme, and sometimes a good deal of merriment was caused by the supposition that Mother might own a top hat, or Father a petticoat; but what a lot of useful words could be introduced to a young child in this way.

Rhymes making use of fingers were always popular.

> *Here is the church, here is the steeple.*
> *Open the doors and there's all the people.*
> *Here is the parson going upstairs.*
> *And here he is a-saying his prayers.*

For this the index finger was covered by a white handkerchief, and the other hand used to provide the church and the stairs. The rhyming of people and steeple occurs in many Sussex folk rhymes.

Many jingles had the feel of nursery rhymes, such as this one from my mother.

> *There was an old woman had three sons,*
> *Jerry, James and John.*
> *Jerry was hung, James was drowned,*
> *John was lost and never was found.*
> *And there was the end of her three sons,*
> *Jerry, James and John.*

The fate of the three sons was not expected to worry a young mind, so even at an early age one was taught the difference between fiction and reality.

Rhymes had many uses. Children used them in the front of their books to persuade others from failing to return them after borrowing.

> *Steal not this book, for fear of shame.*
> *For in it is the owner's name.*
> *And when you're dead the Lord will say*
> *Where is that book you stole away.*

The whole thing was summed up very neatly in this bit of dialect doggerel.

He as takes what isn't hisn
When he's catched, he'll goo to prison.

The early years of the Salvation Army in Sussex were constantly dogged by threats and disturbances. Mrs E Vincent remembered when even quite nice children would happily shout:

Salvation Army
All gone barmy.

Nineteenth century children may have been a little rough and tough at times, but then they grew up in a hard world. Many parents, and most school teachers, believed in the 'spare the rod and spoil the chile' philosophy.

Mother's love is one thing, Father's belt's another.
If you don't get one, you'll sure to get the other.

And even more definite:

> *Down with his trousers and up with his shirt.*
> *And a dozen good strokes will do him no hurt.*

Most girls on leaving school had to go into domestic service, just as most boys went on the land. Young domestic servants were taught how to make a bed with the help of this rhyme:

> *First the foot and then the head,*
> *That's the way to make a bed.*

Almost the only escape from service for the girl was marriage and children. But first she may have managed a few years when the thought of love filled her mind. But there was always someone to bring the starry-eyed one back to earth.

> *False love is plenty, true love is scant.*
> *Love is pleasant when it is new.*
> *But when it's old, it soon grows cold*
> *And fades away like the morning dew.*

Soldiers were always a great attraction, as the girls just couldn't resist a bright uniform. Local lads often missed out in consequence, as these lines from the

Graffham WI Scrapbook illustrate:

> *Polly said she loved me, but she told a fib.*
> *Said that she never loved no other, but she did.*
> *She doted on the bandsman, who played upon the flute.*
> *And every night he charmed her, with his tootle-oddle-oot.*

But soldiers always had a bad reputation as in this rhyme, remembered by my mother:

> *The Royal Sussex is going today,*
> *Leaving the girls in the family way.*

Meanwhile the realities of marriage in a tiny cottage, or perhaps not even that, with a man's wage of twelve and sixpence a week, and a rapidly increasing family, came all too quickly.

> *If you've got one you can run,*
> *If you've got two you may goo,*
> *But if you've got three, you must bide where thee be.*

So beware, girls.

> *If you rock the cradle empty*
> *Then you shall have babies plenty.*

Even when they grew up, they were still a worry.

> *A son's a son 'til he gets him a wife.*
> *A daughter's a daughter all her life.*

Washing day was a weekly chore from which there was no escape. The earlier in the week the better, once Sunday was over.

> *Wash on Monday, all the week to dry.*
> *Wash on Tuesday, not so much awry.*
> *Wash on Wednesday, much to blame,*
> *Wash on Thursday, wash for shame.*
> *Wash on Friday, wash at need,*
> *Wash on Saturday, slut indeed.*

Many young lads, too little for other farm work, were employed as bird scarers. A lonely and soul-destroying job, even on a fine day, but worth a few valuable pence a week. This is a bird scarer's rhyme from around 1800:

> *Shoo all awy, shoo all away,*
> *And don't come back no more today.*
> *For if you do, I'll up with me clappers*
> *And knock you backards.*

There were many rhymes to help the countryman get through his rather humdrum life. For instance, when buying a horse, always remember:

> *One white foot, buy him.*
> *Two white feet, try him.*
> *Three white feet, shy him.*
> *Four white feet, fly him.*

Nature provided many good subjects for rhymes.
> *Beware of the oak, it draws the stroke.*
> *Avoid the ash, it courts the flash.*
> *Creep under the thorn,*
> *It can save you from harm.*

Many of these rhymes contain a lot of truth. For instance:

> *An elder stake and blackthorn ether,*
> *Will make a hedge to last for ever.*

Often heard in Sussex, although certainly not confined to just one county, was the following familiar jingle:

> *Four seeds in a hole,*
> *One for the rook, one for the crow,*
> *One to rot and one to grow.*

This would have been brought out each year as seeds were planted with a dibbling iron, known in Sussex as a dibber.

Huck was the dialect word for a pea-pod, and it occurs in this Sussex children's rhyme:

> *Pea-pod hucks, twenty for a pin.*
> *If you doant like'em, I'll take 'em back agin.*

Evidently this rhyme goes back to the days when pins were given as small change in drapers' shops. Food sometimes features in rhymes, but not always in a joyful sense. Sussex farm boys who boarded at certain farmhouses could have recited a rhyme such as this:

> *Pork and cabbage all the year,*
> *Mouldy bread and stale beer,*
> *Rusty bacon, stinking cheese,*
> *A chaff bed that's full of fleas.*

At the end of the year the parson had to have his tithes, accompanied by the usual grumbling from the farmers:

> *We've cheated the parson, we'll cheat him agin.*
> *For why should the ole vicar have one in ten.*

Drinking was a sure way to forget your troubles. This was said to have been brewed from one bushel of malt:

> *Fifty gallons to turn your cap,*
> *Fifty gallons of worse than that,*
> *Fifty gallons of Tibalty Tink,*
> *Fifty gallons the Devil couldn't drink.*

This is where I will leave these particular rhymes, but if I have not included the ones you recall, please forgive me. If you send them to me I may be able to put them into another book. So remember:

> If 'ifs' and 'buts' were pots and pans
> There'd be no work for tinker-mans.

The last word, some Sussex epitaphs

One would expect that many older Sussex epitaphs would include dialect words, but although there have been many unusual inscriptions noted, actual dialect words are surprisingly rare. Helena Hall, the Lindfield historian, was thrilled to note the word 'fust' on a Lindfield stone – so much so that she had the inscription recut in June 1956 in order to preserve it. She wrote that she thought this was the only instance of dialect on a Sussex tombstone, although she was not entirely correct. The Lindfield inscription reads:

> Long was my pain, great was my grief.
> Surgeons I'd many but no relief.
> I trust through Christ to rise with the just.
> My leg and thigh was buried fust.

But how about this from an inscription in Selmeston church, dated 1639?:

> *The body of Henry Rogers.*
> *A painful preacher in this church two and thirty yeeres.*

The word painful is used in its old Sussex meaning of painstaking.

Perhaps epitaphs should not entertain, but the following, said to have been seen in Ditchling churchyard, is certainly full of humour:

> *Below lies for sartin*
> *Honest old Harting.*
> *And snug, close beside 'im*
> *His fat wife, a wide one.*
> *If another you lack,*
> *Look down and see Jack.*
> *And farther a yard,*
> *Lyes Charles who drank hard.*
> *And near t'un his Moggy,*
> *Who never got groggy.*
> *Like Charles and her Father,*
> *Too abstemious rather,*

And therefore popp'd off,
In a tissicky cough.
Look round now and spy 'bout,
The whole family is laid out.

Tissicky as relating to cough may be translated as troublesome.

The following epitaph on a blacksmith (with slight variations) is often quoted as being used at different times on gravestones at Felpham, Hollington, Westbourne, Sidlesham, Stedham and Mid-Lavant. It also crops up in other counties. Sometimes it is said to have been written by the Sussex poet William Hayley for the grave of William Spray, a Felpham blacksmith, but this would have been impossible date-wise.

My sledge and hammer lie reclined,
My bellows too have lost their wind.
My fire extinct; my forge decay'd,
And in the dust my vice is laid.
My coal is spent, my iron gone.
The nails are druv – my work is done.

It has to be said that most often when this is quoted, the lovely Sussex word *druv* gives way more prosaically to *driven*.

The next one is not exactly dialect, although some of the words have more than one meaning. It was said to have been written by Mr Lee of *The Sussex Express* for the grave of Mr Droyley, an illiterate Lewes horse-dealer.

> *Here lies a man that lived by lying.*
> *Some people thought 'twould leave him dying.*
> *But to the nation's great surprise,*
> *Even in his grave he lies.*

More play on words, for someone named Peck, in an East Sussex churchyard.

> *For forty years Peck bore life's bubbles,*
> *Til death released a peck of troubles.*
> *So fell poor Peck, as all things must,*
> *And here he lies, a peck of dust.*

Lastly the following lines were said to have concluded an epitaph on a well-loved parish clerk, Richard Bassett:

> *His melody was warbled forth as if he had been thumped between the*
> *shoulders with a pair of bellows.*

Whether this was meant as a compliment regarding his vocal powers is uncertain.

Ploughing with oxen in the Cuckmere Valley

Kettle broth and other Sussex delicacies

During most of my grandfather's life he enjoyed the same 'bracfus'. This was a pudding basin filled with plain bread, broken up and sprinkled with salt and pepper, and then covered with hot water. This he consumed with a spoon, calling it Kettle Broth.

Another memory of Kettle Broth comes from my schooldays, when I attended a one-teacher private school at a village a short distance from Horsham. Because I travelled to school each day on the penny bus, I took my midday meal of sandwiches in a fibre attache case, purchased from Woolworths for sixpence. The school master, evidently for reasons of economy, always had Kettle Broth for his midday repast. This he enjoyed standing over me, as I sat eating my slightly more sophisticated meal. I always wished for an umbrella for the tiny amounts of water and soggy bread showering down on me which did not improve my sandwiches.

Jean Sunderland told me how the broth was made by her grandmother, who added good dollops of farm butter, and sometimes even dripping or cheese. Another version was made with bread, cocoa and sugar. This sounds much nearer to my own mother's favourite 'bread and milk', which was always her recipe for anyone with a sore throat. Another similar dish consisted of a large boiled onion, also with bread, butter, salt and pepper, and covered with hot water, served in a basin. This was considered effective for a tissicky cough.

Some of the above sound reasonalby appetising, but I have always been less enthusiastic over a drink known as Donkey Tea. This was made with dark toast broken up in a cup or glass and covered with hot water. The toast pieces were then strained out. It was often given to children to drink. Tea was once very expensive, so a drink like this, served with sugar, was considered a good substitute.

Several older folk have told me about Peg Nuts or Pig Nuts. Sid Neve said that as a boy in Ninfield he would locate the plant without difficulty using a penknife and going down four to six inches. The 'nut' was at the base of a long slender root. These were regarded as great delicacies, although parents disagreed, saying that such things would give the boys worms. Later Sid found the plant listed under the alternative title of Earth Nut, an umbelliferous white flowered plant with a two-lobed tuberous rootstock.

Mabs Bryant said that she remembered them in the churchyard at Shipley, and that they were very sweet to eat, but only available in the spring. Charlie Potter of Horsham said that with other boys he would go to the Jews Meadows to search for the Peg Nuts. They had tops like carrots, and only needed to be pulled out of the ground.

Marjorie Baldwin of Colgate said they tasted like chestnuts, although the flavour was more delicate. She thought they were sometimes called Pig Nuts as pigs once nosed for them, as they do for truffles.

Every now and then someone asks me if I know anything about Bee Wine. This has nothing to do with bees, but it was certainly very popular in Sussex, and I can remember my grandparents and parents making and drinking it. The 'Bees' were sometimes called Holy Bees or Jerusalem Bees, and to make the drink you needed a 'starter' from someone else (actually it was a yeast culture). This was placed in water and left on a warm window-sill to ferment. The Bees were the small blobs which surfaced and sank repeatedly as the process continued. The wine then had to be fed with demarara sugar and/or sliced lemons. It tasted rather like sweet ginger beer and was extremely palatable. The craze for passing on a starter to a friend went on for some time, but eventually it died out, particuarly as there was a rumour that some folk had become ill through drinking too much of it. The origin of the name Holy or Jerusalem seems completely obscure, although I have heard it said that the names originated because you either drank it or made it on a Sunday.

Block Ornaments were small pieces of meat which had been sliced off when the butcher was making up an order. They were pushed to one side of the chopping board until someone came in and asked for a bag of block ornaments. Doris Hall of Westmeston told me that her mother cooked these welcome oddments of meat gently in water for about half an hour. They were then set aside to allow the fat to harden. This was used to make a dripping cake. The meat pieces were used in a suet crust, providing a cheap meal, with the liquid being used as a base for soup. As they said, 'nuffin' was wasted.

One more memory of hard-times food. Here is a story which may make you cringe. It concerns a labourer known as Ratty, and his family, on a South Downs farm in the nineteenth century. The reason for his nickname was not hard to find, as when threshing was taking place, many rats were disturbed and were killed as they tried to make their escape. At the end of the day Ratty would collect them and take them home. Here they would be skinned by his wife, and made into puddings. He contended that as the rats fed on corn, they were perfectly clean and edible.

*O*ld George and the Horned Devil

A few years ago the *West Sussex Gazette* published a series of stories which I had written about a likeable rogue – Old George – who lived in Brigley, a fictional West Sussex village in the 1920s. For those who are still interested in the doings of Old George and his cronies, here is a new story about him. These tales are, of course, not written in dialect, although the narrator does lapse into a number of dialect words from time to time.

Setting in the corner most nights in The Grapes, I watches our little village world go by. Mostly nothing happens, but every now and again something crops up sto disturb our quiet lives. I'm not too sure why it should be, but somehow when these little bits of excitement occured, there always seems to be one perticular person in the middle of it all. Yes, you must have guessed – it's Old George. More often than not it tends to be George putting one across the rest of the regulars in the pub, or at anywise deciding that he has done so according to his own judgement. But jest once in a whiles the old rogue slips up, and he ends up holding the dirty end of the stick, as 'twere. This is one of those rare occasions.

You may remember that Old George took hisself a lodger awhile ago, a preaching feller. Well that didn't pan out too well, so you would think he had learnt his lesson.

But no, once agin he announces with that familiar 'I know what I'm doing' sort of voice, that he has another lodger moving in. This time its a gent from Lunnon who wants to study Sussex folklore. Well most of the regulars didn't have a clue as to what George meant by this, and I'm fairly sartin that he really didn't know hisself – although he wasn't going to let on any such thing. But we all waited for the Saturday night when the man hisself, Mr Henry Branklin-Hardy, was due to put in an appearance.

Well this was a bit of a let-down, as in spite of his double-barrelled name, he was a small and weedy little tibster of a man, dressed in a set of clothes what looked as if they might have come from one of Farmer Cathchpole's scarecrows. The only fairly new article of clothing he had was a bright orange titfer, which he appeared to be very fond of, as he never removed it from his head all the evening. But we all knew he was a real genelman, as apart from his name, he bought everybody their favourite tipple, and unlike George's last lodger, he didn't mind knocking back quite a few pints hisself.

Nothing much happened for a few days, apart from Henry B-H being seen dorming around the village in the daytime, not doing any harm. But this didn't last long, as he soon started chiping to people in the street, or even asking if he could visit them in their houses. We all thought this a bit of a licker, as we mostly didn't rackon to go into other folks pleaces, until we had both lived in the village for a tidy few years. But we put this strange behaviour down to him coming from Lunnon, where

I supposes they don't know any better.

He even seemed keen to visit Old Mother Heppel, whereas anyone could have told him that you didn't go into her house – not unless you were prepared to come out with a few unwelcome things that you hadn't got on you afore you went in. All the same he seemed pleased with hisself, and it was at this time that we noticed that he appeared to be writing things down in a lil old black book that he carried around with him.

Now the villagers may be a bit slow on the uptake, but it didn't take them too long to realise that what he wanted were any kind of strange titbits of information about the village, in fact the stranger the better. And more to the point, he were prepared to pay for this information. Of course, once this had sunk in, people like the Shaggs and the Muggeridges, lost no time in thinking up the most weird bits of gossip – all of which he promptly jots down in his lil book. Well that was alright for them as had good imaginations, but others couldn't think of much, so there was soon a 'waiting list' as it were, for the Big Book of Fairy Tales, which our school teacher, Eleanor Twippet, kept on top of her pianner. I'm sure he must have wondered why Jack the Giant Killer and The Sleeping Beauty featured so often in the traditional lore of a West Sussex village.

Well it wasn't jest stories he were after. Apparently he wanted songs as well, perticuly old ballets. As he was George's lodger, George felt he had first claim on the wind-up phonograph machine which he had brought with him. Now George had a reputation as a singer. That is to say, a very bad reputation. The only reason why the Christmas wassailers wanted George to join them was because as soon as he started to sing, someone was sure to offer them a substantial bribe to go and perform in the next street. But this didn't appear to worry Henry too much, in fact he was heard to remark that what we had always thought was George's complete lack of musical talent, was in reality his rare ability to sing in antique modes.

Although most of what was being noted down by our visitor was really a load of nonsense, the village does have a genuine piece of folklore. This is the belief that the old Devil hisself makes an appearance in the churchyard on Midsummer Eve, June 23. Of course, George was not backwards in telling Henry all about this, with suitable embellishments of his own devising. As the appointed date drew near, George offered to escort his lodger to the churchyared on the special evening, and to find him a place where he could hide hisself. Not that George, or in fact anyone else in the village, had ever seen the apparition on the night in question, but that wasn't going to prevent them laying on a good show for the visitor. Just to spice things up a bit, George also mentioned that a few assorted fairies were likely to appear on the same night.

Come the evening, and George and Henry had hid themselves in a suitable place, to await the midnight hour. Strangely enough there appeared to be a few other folks around as well, doing their best to keep out of sight, although what they hoped to see, goodness knows. Well the midnight chimes had just sounded from the old church clock, and nothing appeared to be happening, when suddenly there was a rush of air and a devilish looking thing with a pair of evil horns appeared and made straight for Henry, seemingly attracted by his bright yellow cap. Henry, closely followed by George, didn't wait to discuss the folklorish aspects of the apparition, but put as much space between themselves and the churchyard as they could.

The next night in The Grapes, George was disgustedly denouncing the person who had let loose Saul Champion's bad tempered old goat, with a reputation for hating anything yellow. Apparently Henry had blamed George for the whole thing, and had left the following morning, conveniently forgetting to pay George the rent he owed him.

Old George's particular mate, Chubber Holman, was unwise enough to enquire from George as to who had set the goat free. Before he could reply, someone tactlessly suggested that it must have bin the fairies – but that person made sure he was well out of the door before George could reach him.

Two letters in dialect

Just to prove that, even in relatively modern times, the art of Sussex dialect has not been lost, here are parts of two letters written to Sussex newspapers. Both the writers are no longer with us, but I hope their shades will look with approval on my reprint of these gems of Sussex wisdom.

The first was printed in the *West Sussex Gazette* back in 1957, and was written by WG Daish, a well-known expert on Sussex speech (he wrote three important articles unter the title *The Voice of Sussex* for the *Sussex County Magazine* in 1956). Stanley Godman, himself no stranger to Sussex dialect, had written an article for the *Gazette* on James Richards, the Sussex dialect poet. The following is part of Mr Daish's comment in verse on this article.

> *Yest'dy raglar as a clock,*
> *De o'd Wes Sussex come along;*
> *So down I sets to git a look,*
> *En see what news from home she brung.*
>
> *I looks to Horsham fust, yore sure.*
> *To find out how me clawneys be,*

Afore I turns de page fur more,
O' things dat means so much to me.

I warnt aaf pleased to see yore bit,
Right in de place whur she belongs,
'Bout all de Sussex talk en wit,
Of o'd Mus' Richards en he's songs.

Clawneys are family relations.

The second extract was written by a good friend of mine, Frank Holmes of Horsham, to The West Sussex County Times in the 1970s. The paper had commented on an old Sussex jibe mentioned in one of my own books, suggesting that some of the girls of Horsham's past were of doubtful virtue. His letter began:

Tiz noe good you tryin' to tell oi 'bout them 'orsam gells bein' noe better'n they shud be, coz what young Tony Wales sez in 'is book, it be trew an' I can pruv it.

It do sim thet Vicar, not young Peter, but a chep called Matthew Alwyne, 'ee were worritin' 'bout 'em tidy bit, so 'ee ups and goes to 'orsam Assizes, and 'ee do go on a bit at Jury there, tellin' a fair ole tale to em 'bout the carryins on.

Twas on 12th July 1602, and I got it writ down 'ere. Ee sez to em, ee sez, an' I copys this 'ere bit – 'That within the last few years, two or three harlots in his Parish have had bastards and suffered no punishment other than excommunication. At this time, two of them have three bastards, and a third is pregnant.'

So yew git outa that if ee ken. Doan ee be sayin' what ant trew. You be wrong, and young Tony, ee be right fer once.

The old well at Findon, c1900

Acknowledgements

C Anscombe, G Attrill, Mrs Axtell, Miss M Baldwin, Mrs M Bryant, Mrs C Chandler, S Copinger, CW Cramp, Mrs Fyfield, Mr and Mrs Garner, Miss D Hall, G Hall, Mrs P Harrison, Mrs Holden, F Holmes, LE Jenner, Miss Marshall, Mrs I Maulden, Miss V Mercer, AA Moore, H Mousdell, Mrs M Murray, S Neve, D Nicholls, HA Pearce, Mrs P Phillips, C Potter, Mrs E Powell, H Rapley, Miss A Robinson, Miss M Robinson, Mrs D Sargent, Mrs J Sunderland, B Taberner, Mr Taylor, G Townsend, Mrs F Tuts, Mrs E Vincent, Mrs C Wales, H Wales, Mrs H Wales, Mrs M Wales, R Wales, Mrs Wheatley, Mrs W Whiting.

Some of the above good folk are no longer with us, but they are included in the list as a small mark of respect to their memory.

The acknowledgements are certainly not complete, as much of the material in this book has been culled from my notebooks going back over the past half century; also some information has been given to me in hurried conversations at the end of my talks.

Bibliography and references

Ashington Village Memories, WI
Beckett, Arthur, *The Spirit of the Downs*, 1909
　　　　　The Wonderful Weald, 1911
　　　　　Adventures of a Quiet Man, 1933
Burstow, Henry, *Reminiscences of Horsham*, 1911
Coleman, S Jackson, *Sussex in Vignette*, ND
Copper, Bob, *Early to Rise*, 1976
Duggan Rees, J, Slindon, *Portrait of a Sussex Village*, 1988
Goldsworthy, Margaret (ed), *Sussex Bedside Anthology*, 1950
Gosset, AL, *Shepherds of Britain*, 1911
Julyan, HE, *Rottingdean*, 1948
Lower, Richard, *Tom Cladpole's Jurney to Lunnon*
　　　　　Jan Cladpole's Trip to 'Merricur
in Search of Dollar Trees
Meynell, Esther, *Country Ways*, 1942
Parish, WD, *Dictionary of the Sussex Dialect*, 1875
Richards, J, *De Good News According to Mark*, 1936
Unwin, Mrs Cobden, *The Hungry Forties*, ND
Whitechurch, VL, *Downland Echoes*, 1924
Wisborough Green Village Book, WI

Many Sussex newspapers, particularly the *West Sussex Gazette* and the *West Sussex County Times*. Magazines including *Evergreen, Petworth Society Magazine, Sussex Life* and the journal of the Sussex Archaeological Society. I am also vastly indebted to the old *Sussex County Magazine* and its many contributors.

About the author

Tony Wales was born in Horsham in 1924 and has lived there for most of his life. Originally he worked in the music business, becoming Press and Publications Officer of the English Folk Dance and Song Society at its national headquarters, Cecil Sharp House, in London. After nearly twenty years, during which time he compiled many books on folk music, he moved on to become the London manager of the American Library of Congress.

After retirement Tony ran his own academic book selling business for several years. For some twenty-five years he has also been writing books on Sussex folklore and old country life.

Tony Wales's previous titles are:

We Wunt be Druv, 1976

A Sussex Garland, 1979

A Day Out in Old Sussex, 1982

Long Summer Days, 1983

The West Sussex Village Book, 1984, revised 1999

Ballads, Bands and Bellringers, 1985

Horsham in Old Picture Postcards
Vol 1, 1987, *Vol 2*, 1992

An Album of Old Horsham, 1989

Sussex Customs, Curiosities and Country Lore, 1990

Sussex Ghosts and Legends, 1992

Littlehampton in Old Picture Postcards, 1993

Horsham and District in Old Photographs, 1994

Landscapes of West Sussex, 1994

Photo Archive Series: Brighton and Hove, 1997;
Bognor Regis, 1997; *Hastings*, 1998

Horsham Then and Now, 2000

A Treasury of Sussex Folklore, 2000

Ploughing near the Long Man of Wilmington, September 1907

S.B. Publications *publish a wide range of books on Sussex and other counties of England covering aspects of local history, guides and walking books.*

For a catalogue please write to:

SB Publications
19 Grove Road
Seaford
East Sussex BN25 1TP

or access us through our web site:

www.sbpublications.swinternet.co.uk